I0814689
THIS JOURNAL BELONGS TO

Published by Yellow Pear Press, an imprint of Mango Publishing, a division of Mango Publishing Group, Inc.

Cover Design: Elina Diaz
Cover photo: Niki Irving
Layout & Design: Elina Diaz

For permission requests, please contact the publisher at:
Mango Publishing Group
2850 S Douglas Road, 4th Floor
Coral Gables, FL 33134 USA
info@mango.bz

For special orders, quantity sales, course adoptions and corporate sales, please email the publisher at sales@mango.bz. For trade and wholesale sales, please contact Ingram Publisher Services at: customer.service@ingramcontent.com or +1.800.509.4887.

Flourish and Bloom Journal: A Cute Notebook of Buds, Blossoms, and Petals

ISBN: (print) 978-1-64250-960-1
BISAC category code: NON000000, NON-CLASSIFIABLE

yellow pear press

CPSIA information can be obtained
at www.ICGtesting.com
Printed in the USA
JSHW051420030323
38472JS00004B/26

9 781642 509601